AF479962

KEMANI'S GRAPHICS BAND

Artist

Kemani Telfer

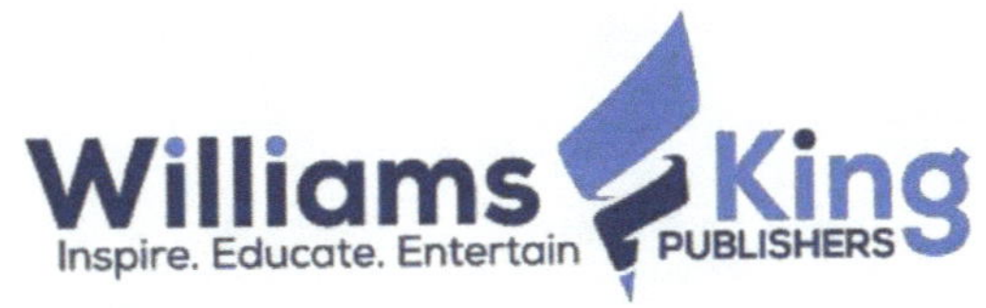

Kemani Telfer

I was inspired to begin drawing by watching my brother draw and, of course, my family encouraging me. Indulging myself with my artwork brings a better connection of good memories for me. For example, the illustration called Camille was inspired when we saw a guy riding on the back of a camel.

When people look at my drawings, I would like them to see and feel a connection of love, freedoms, and bright memories of the joyful times.

Broken Cattle

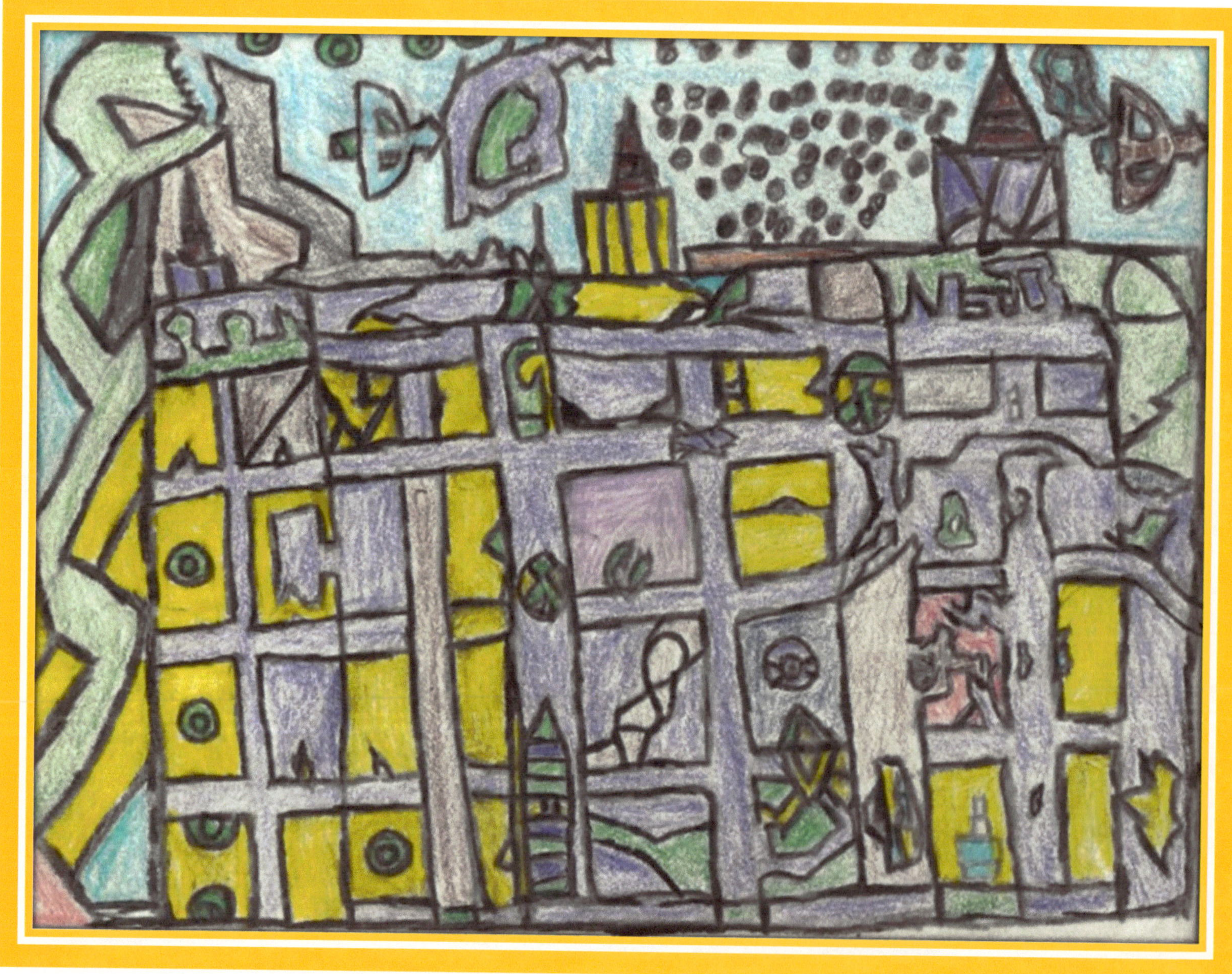

My childhood when there was a hurricane and we had to build something to balance the house.

The Temple

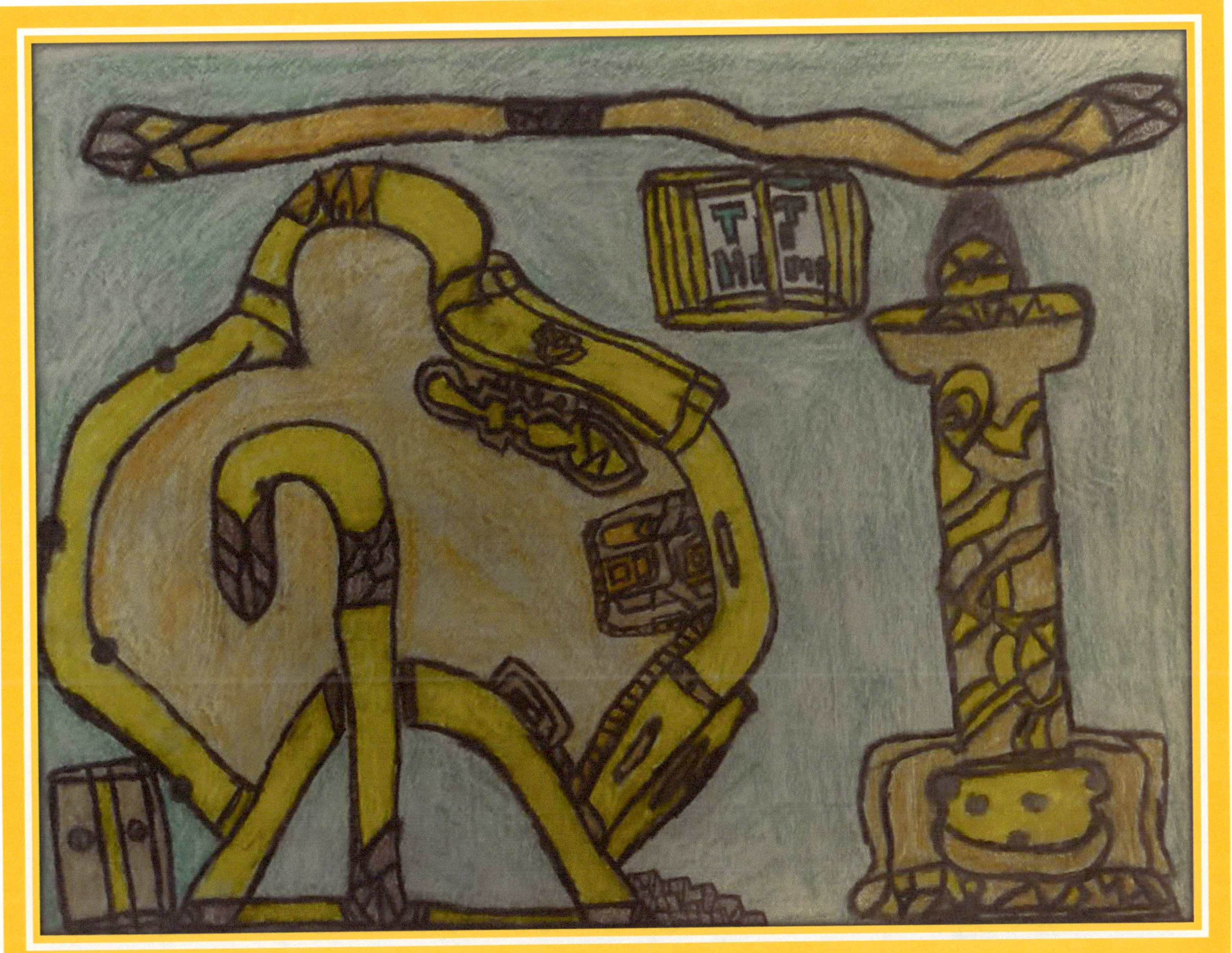

Guard Cattle

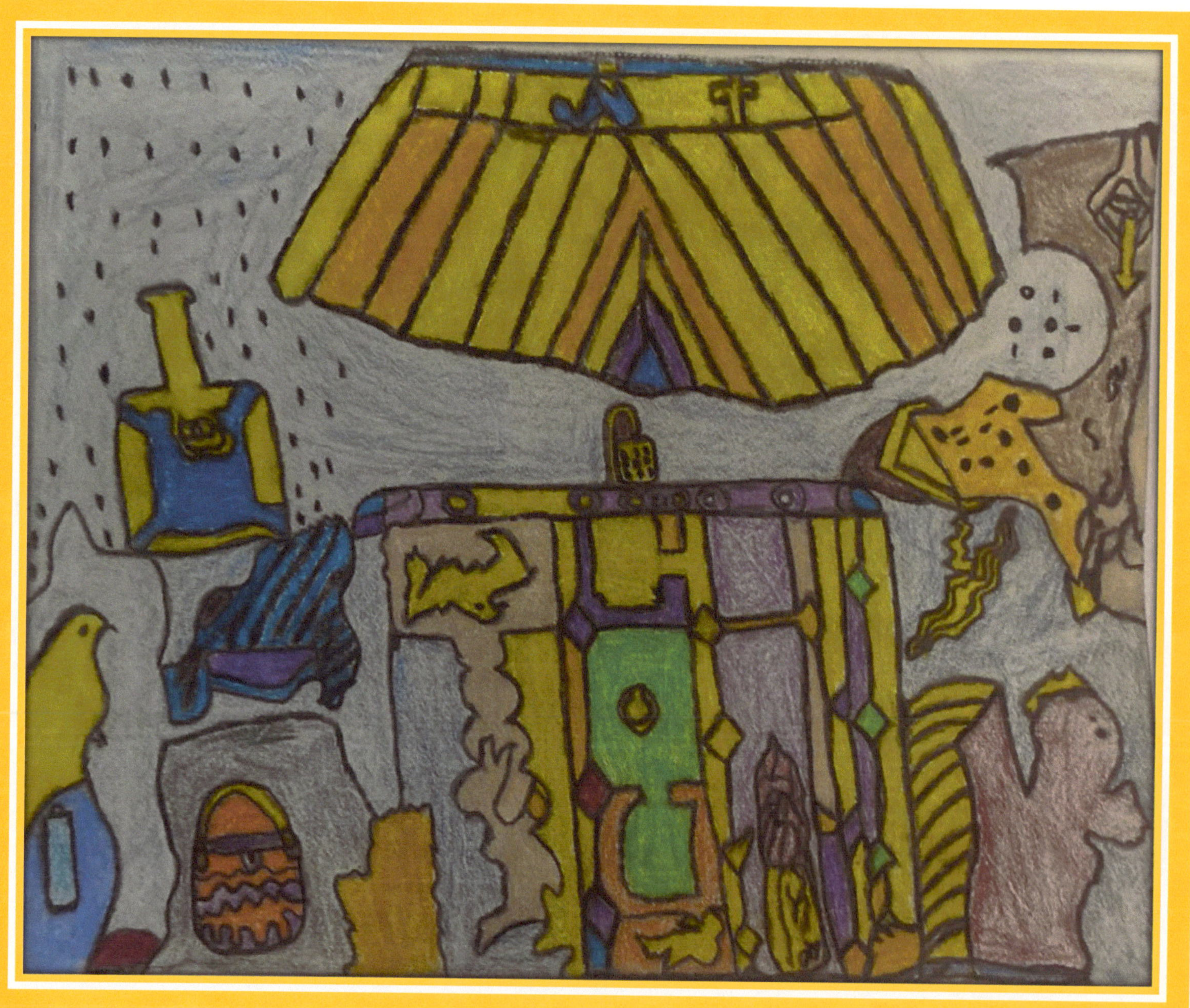

Horse Bridge

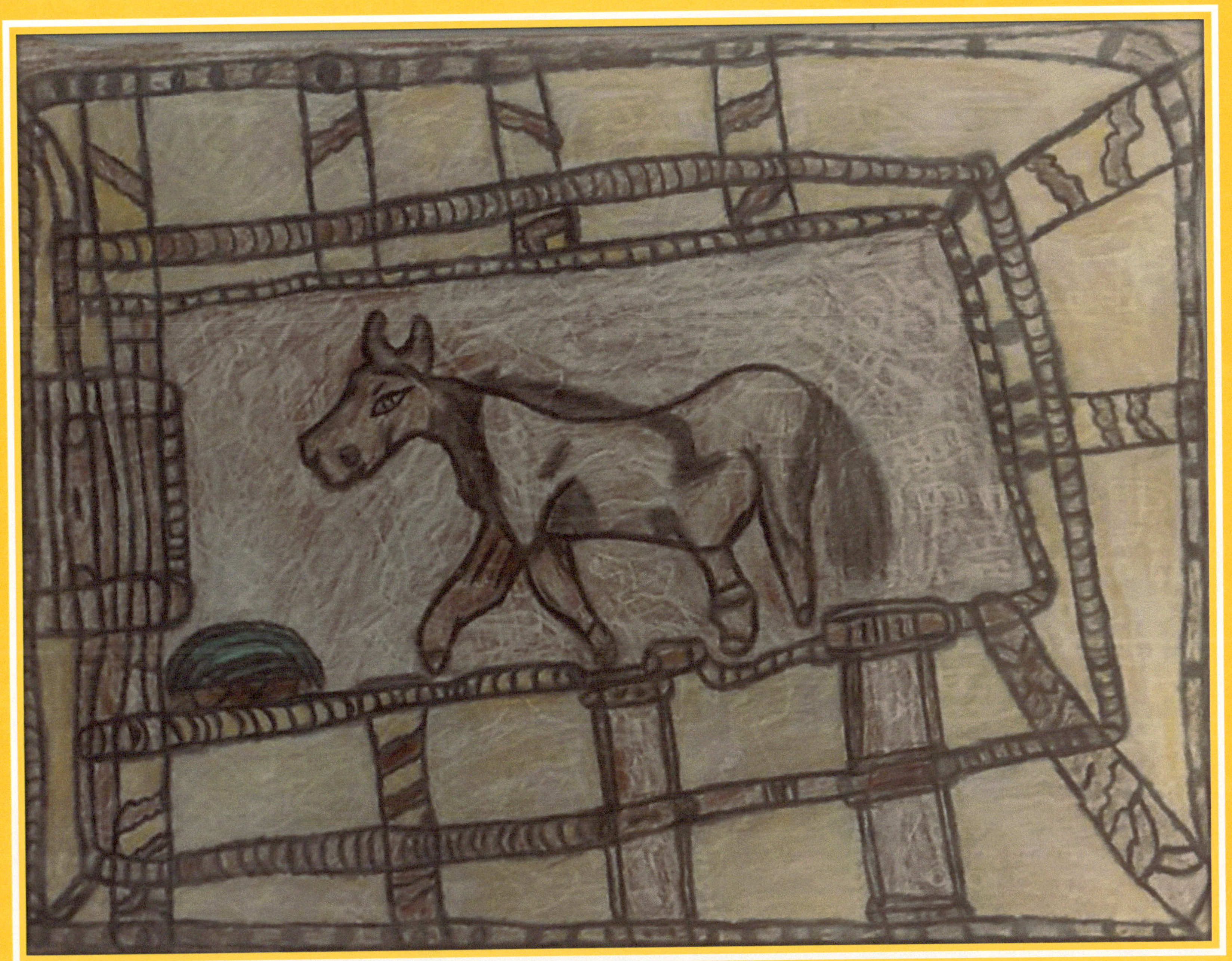

Meditation of Love

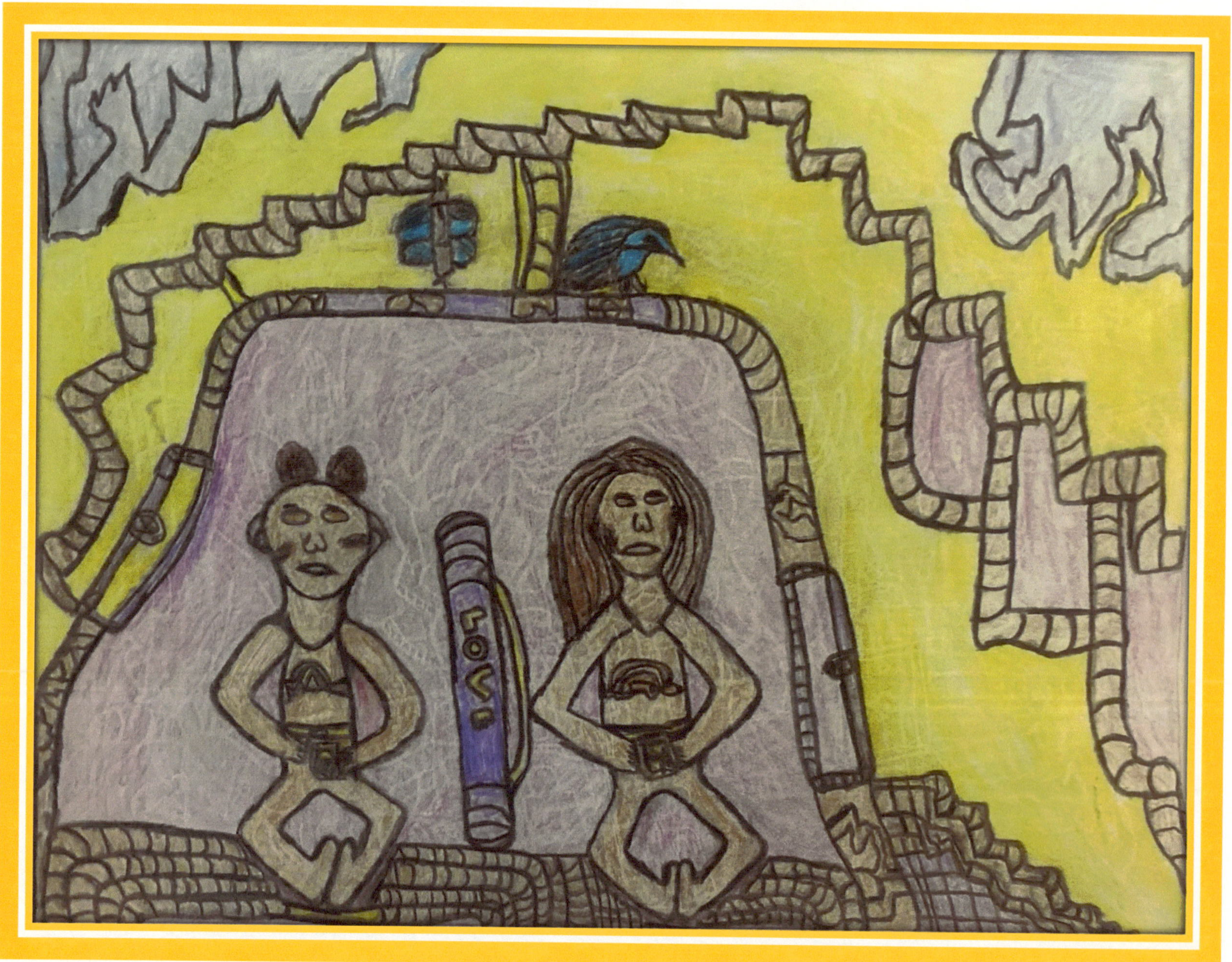

Forest Leader

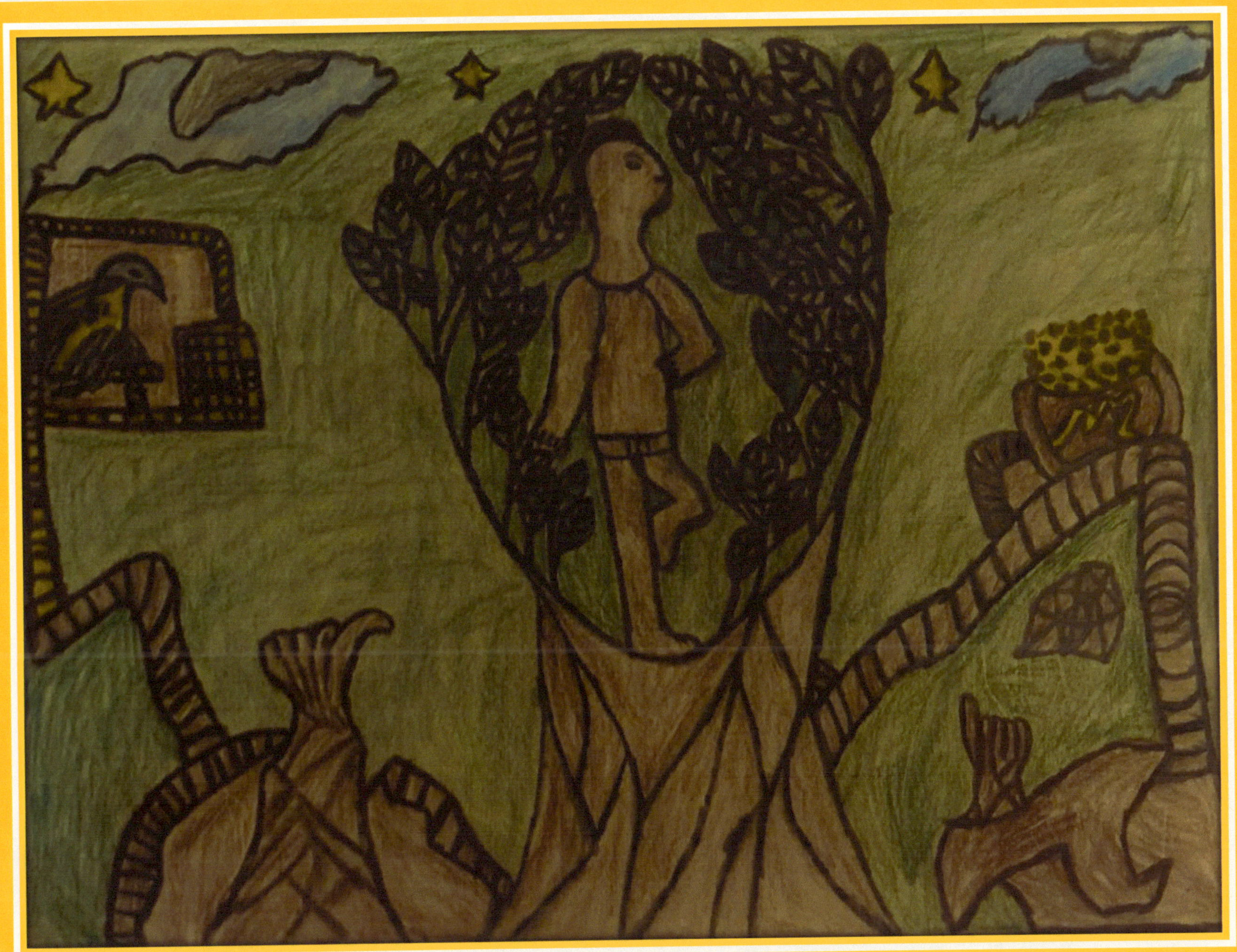

Water Duck

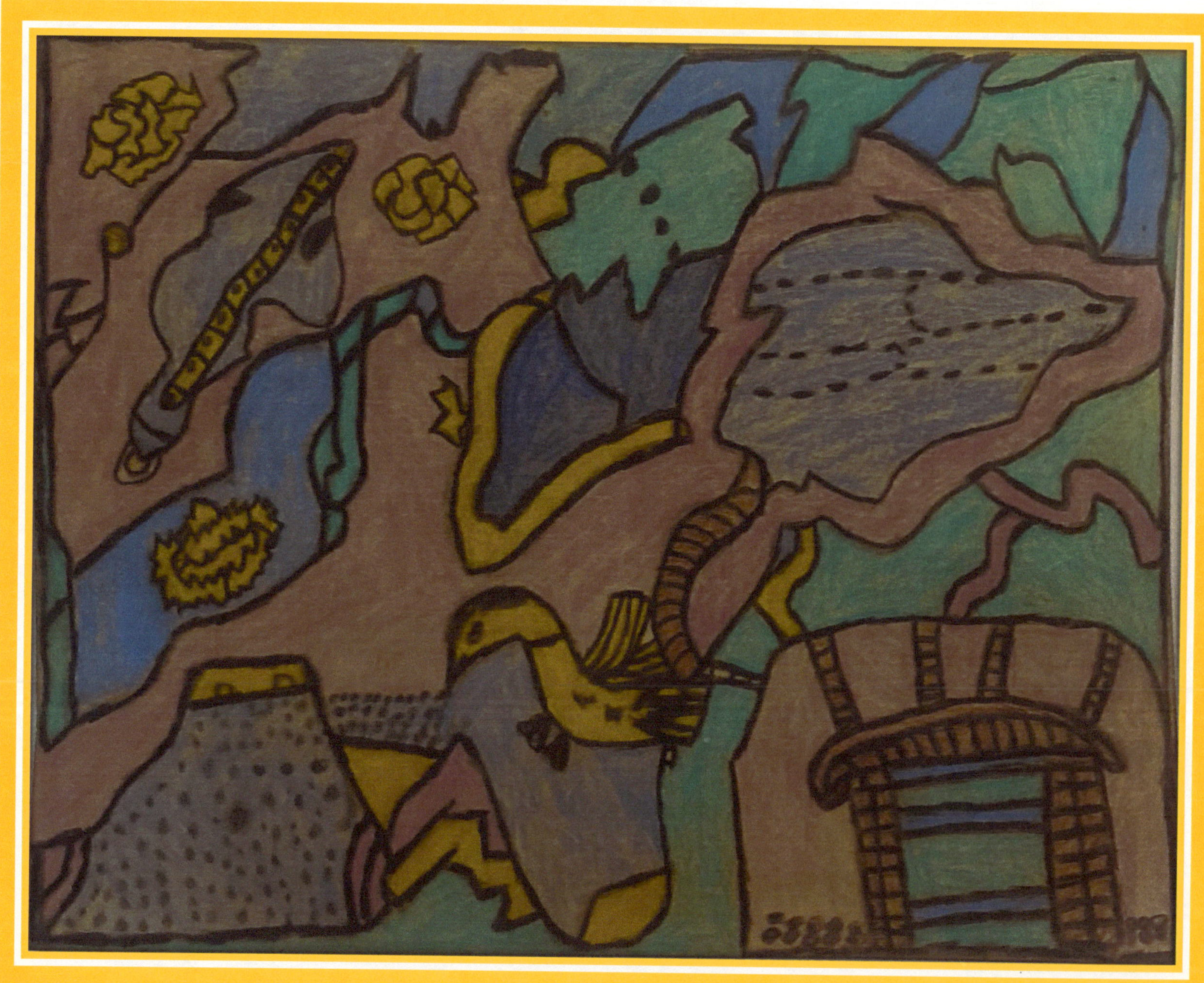

Jenne's Palace

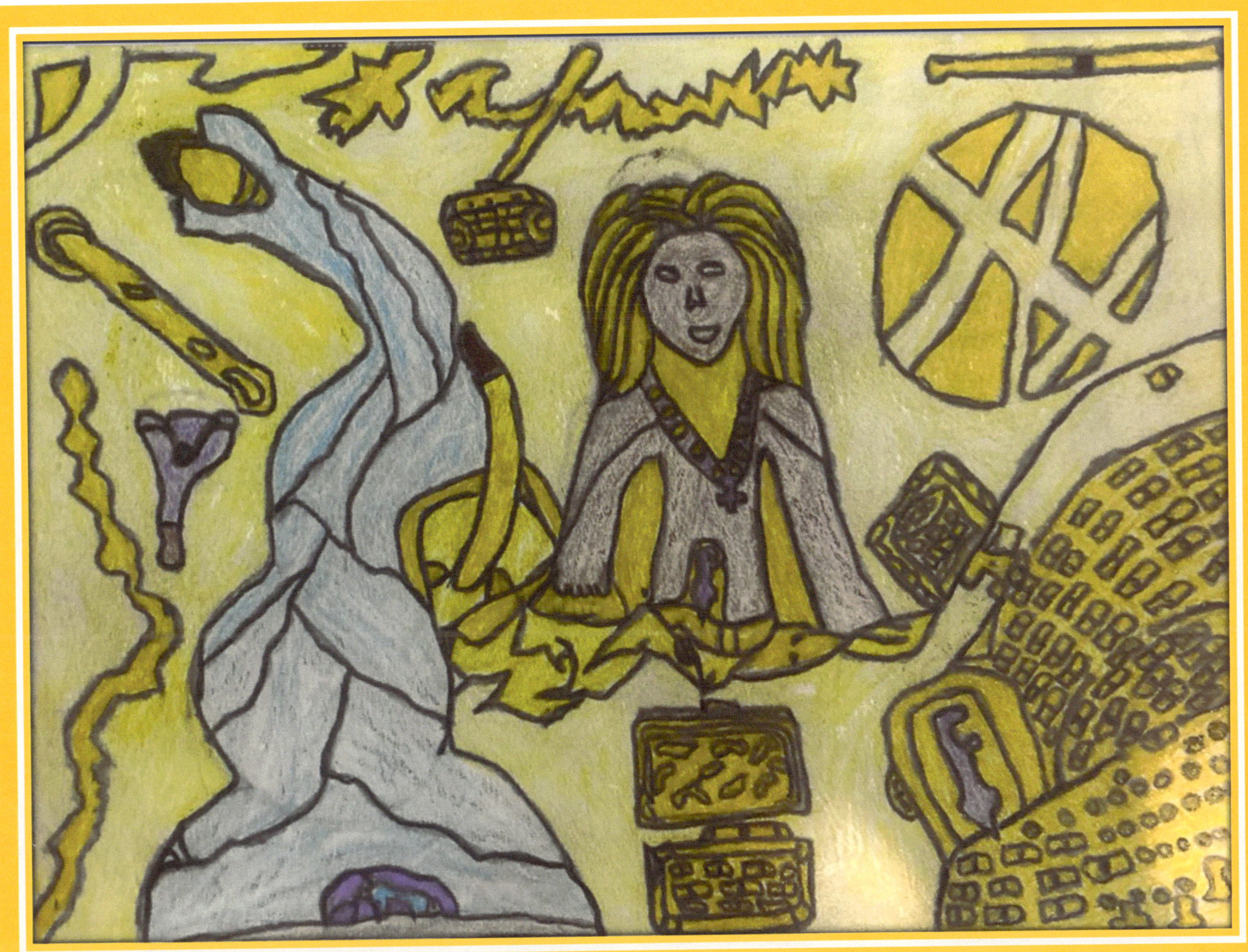

Nat Tycoon

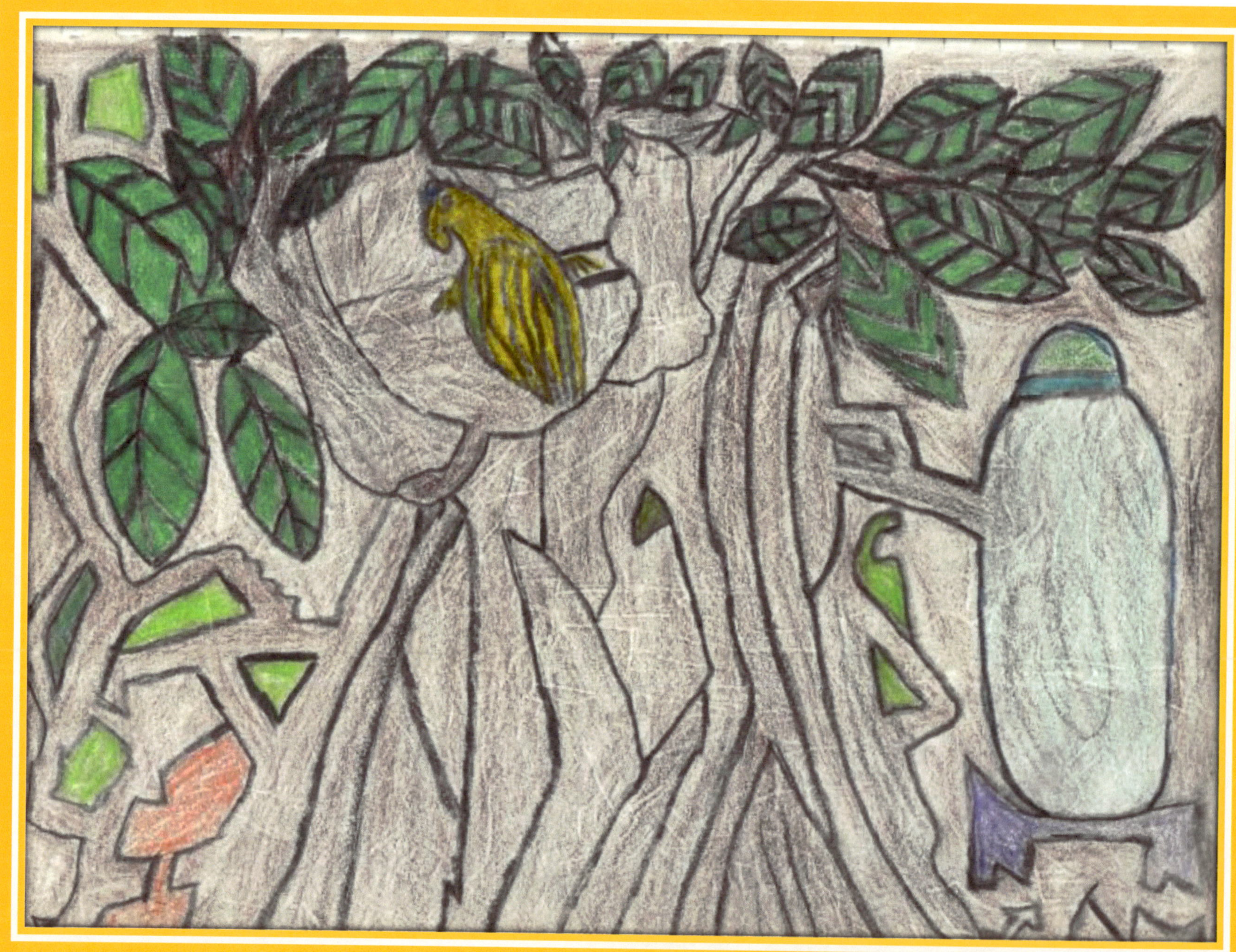

Trap Oran

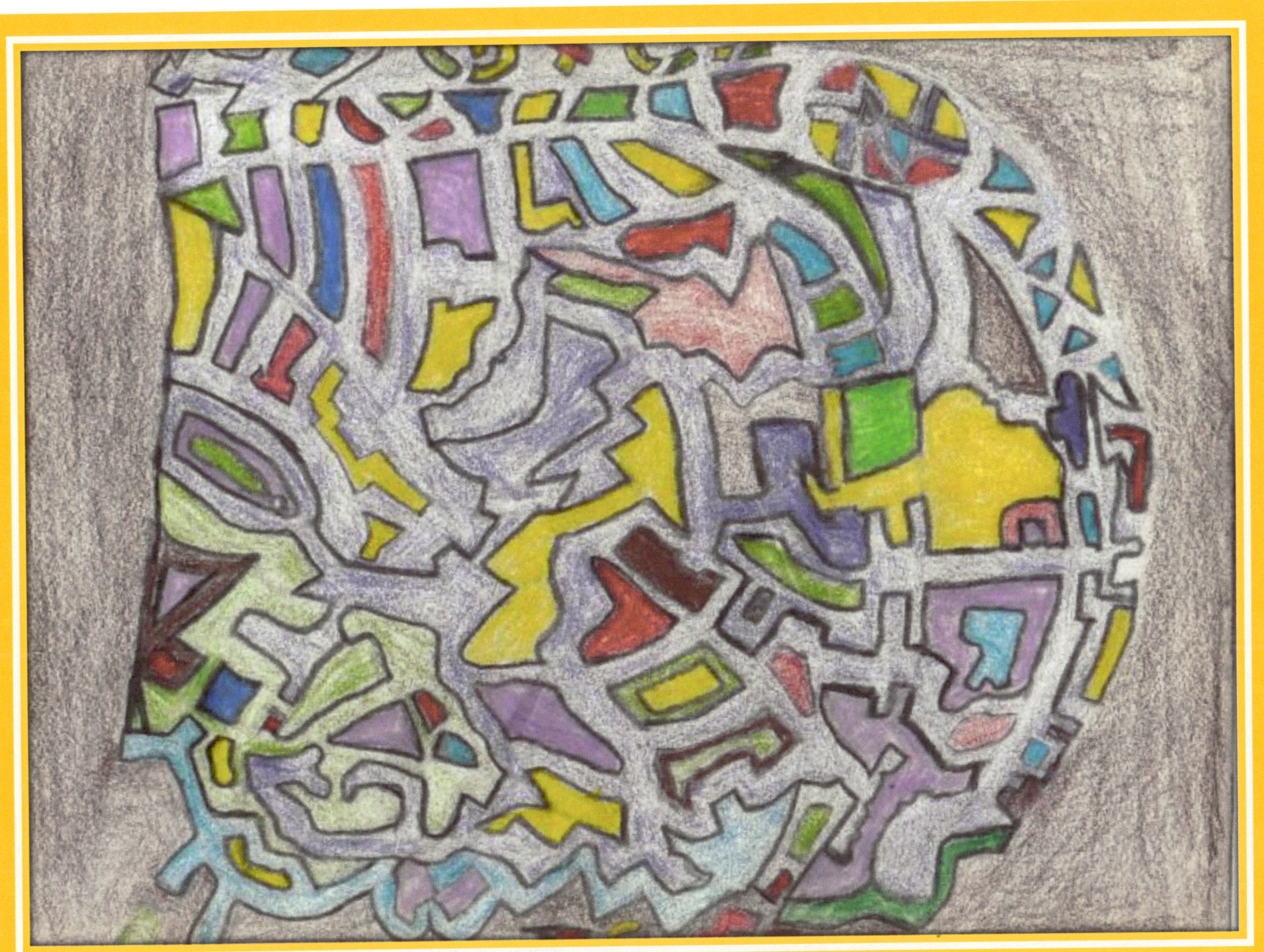

Rangeland

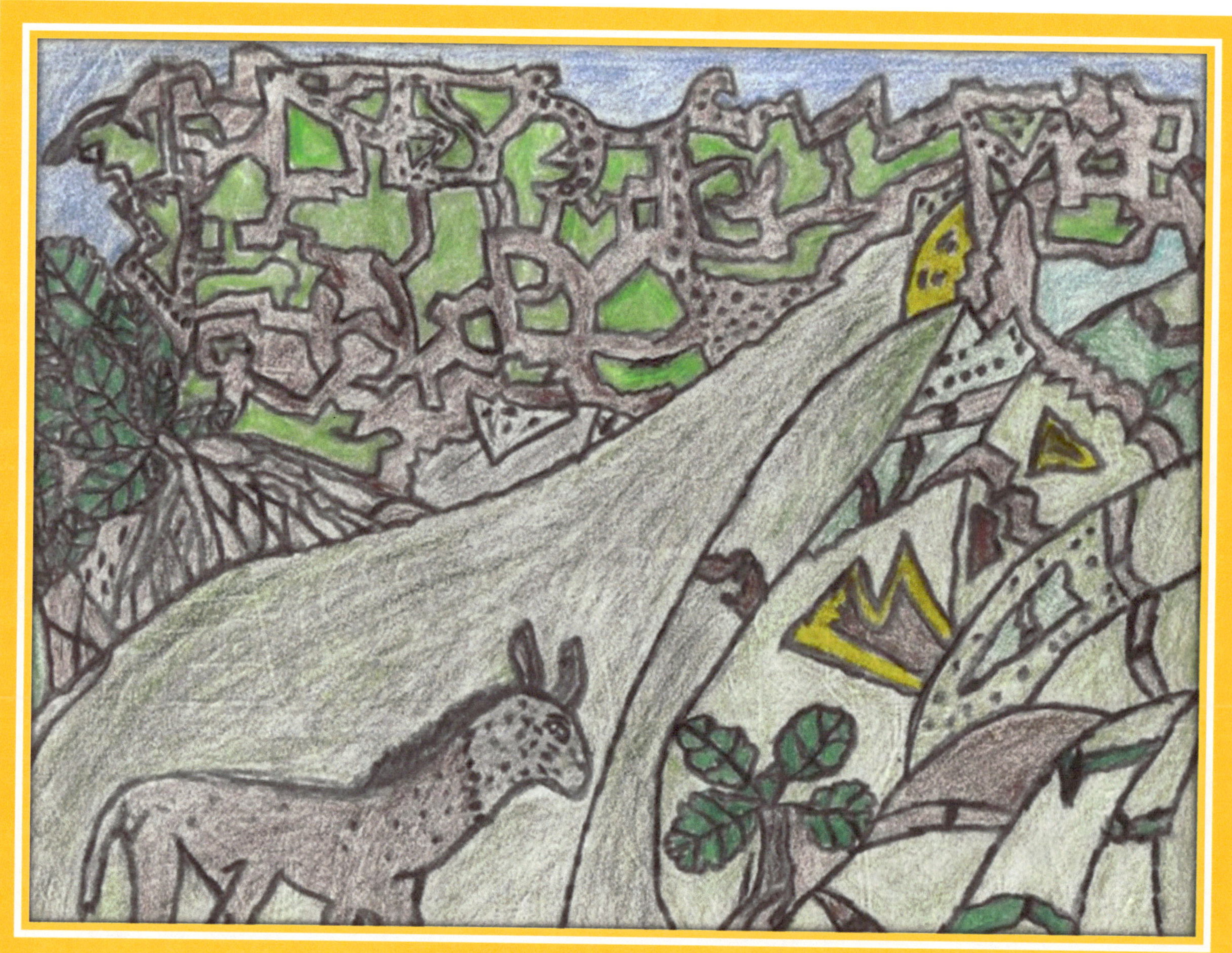

Wild deer looking for a comfortable place.

Space Drive

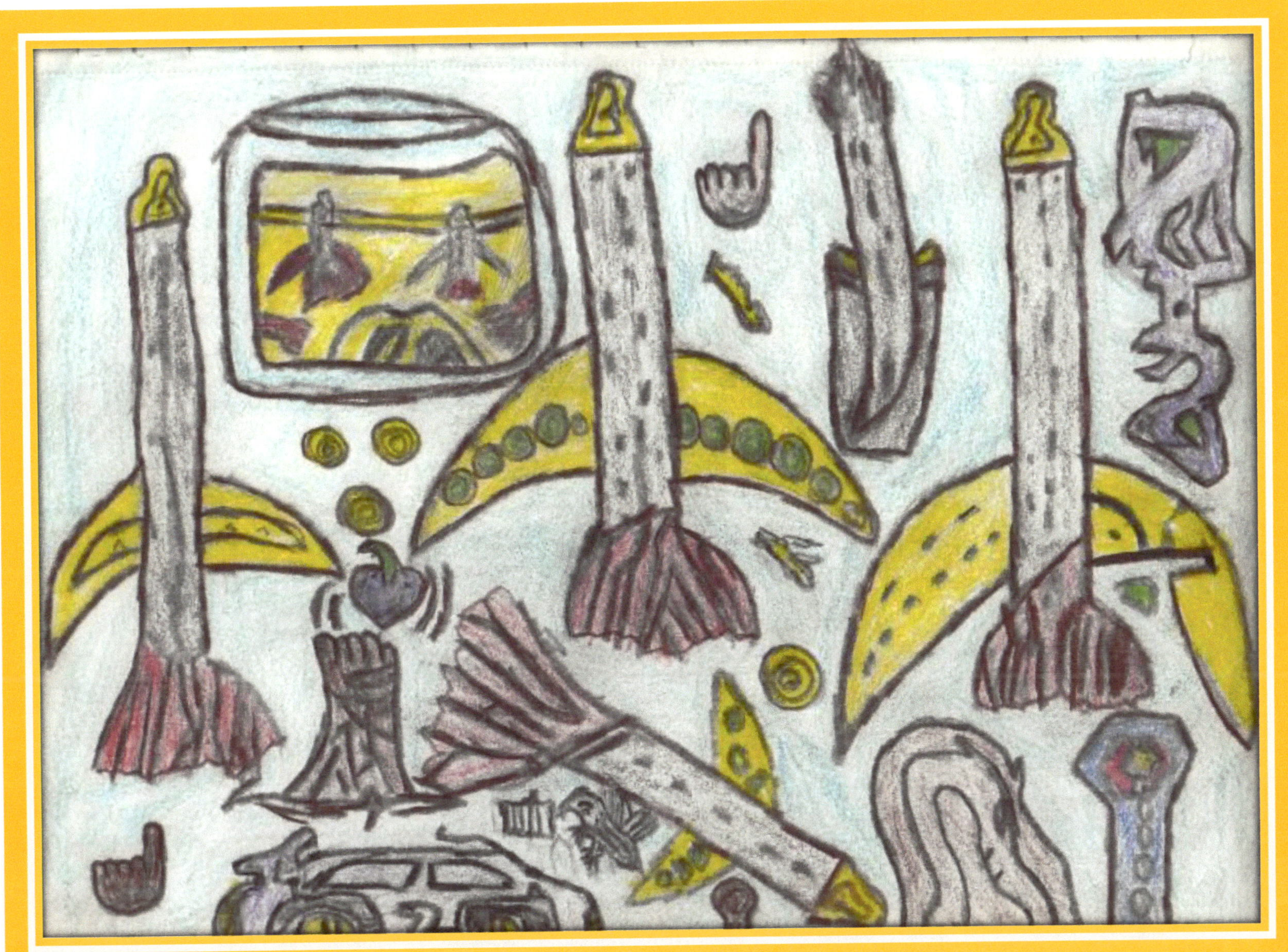

Eyes of the future.

Fire of High

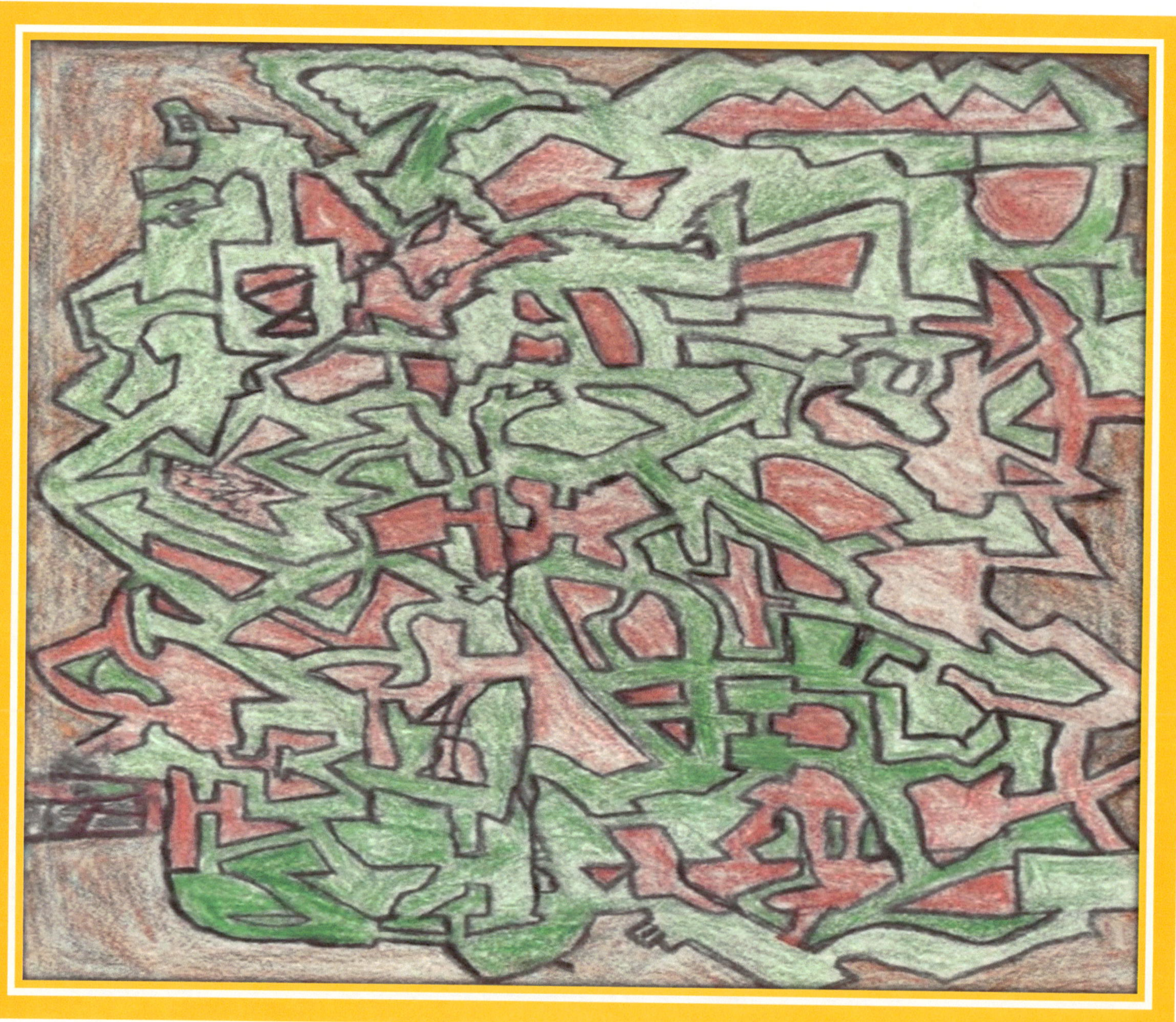

Jungle Duck

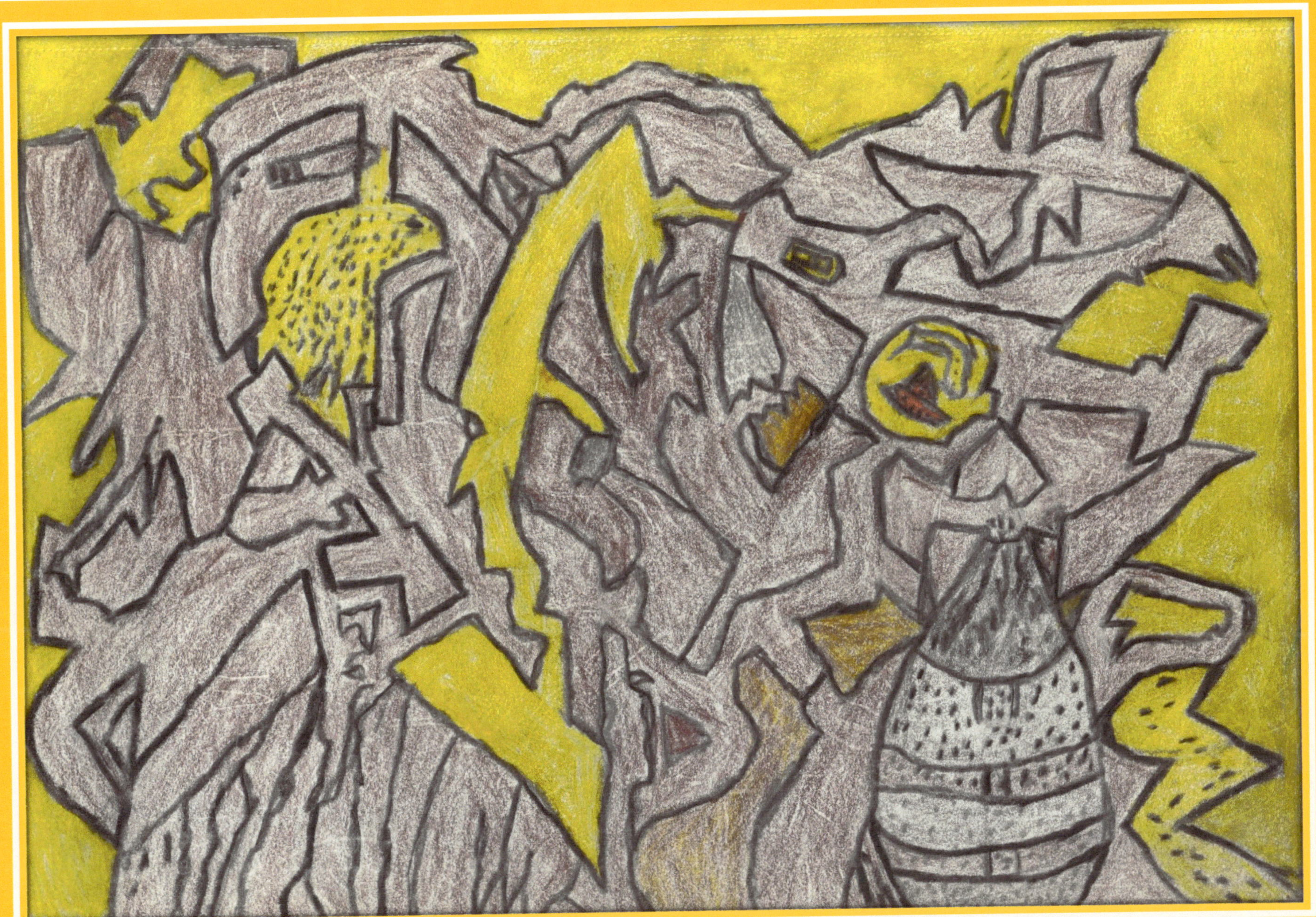

Ancient River

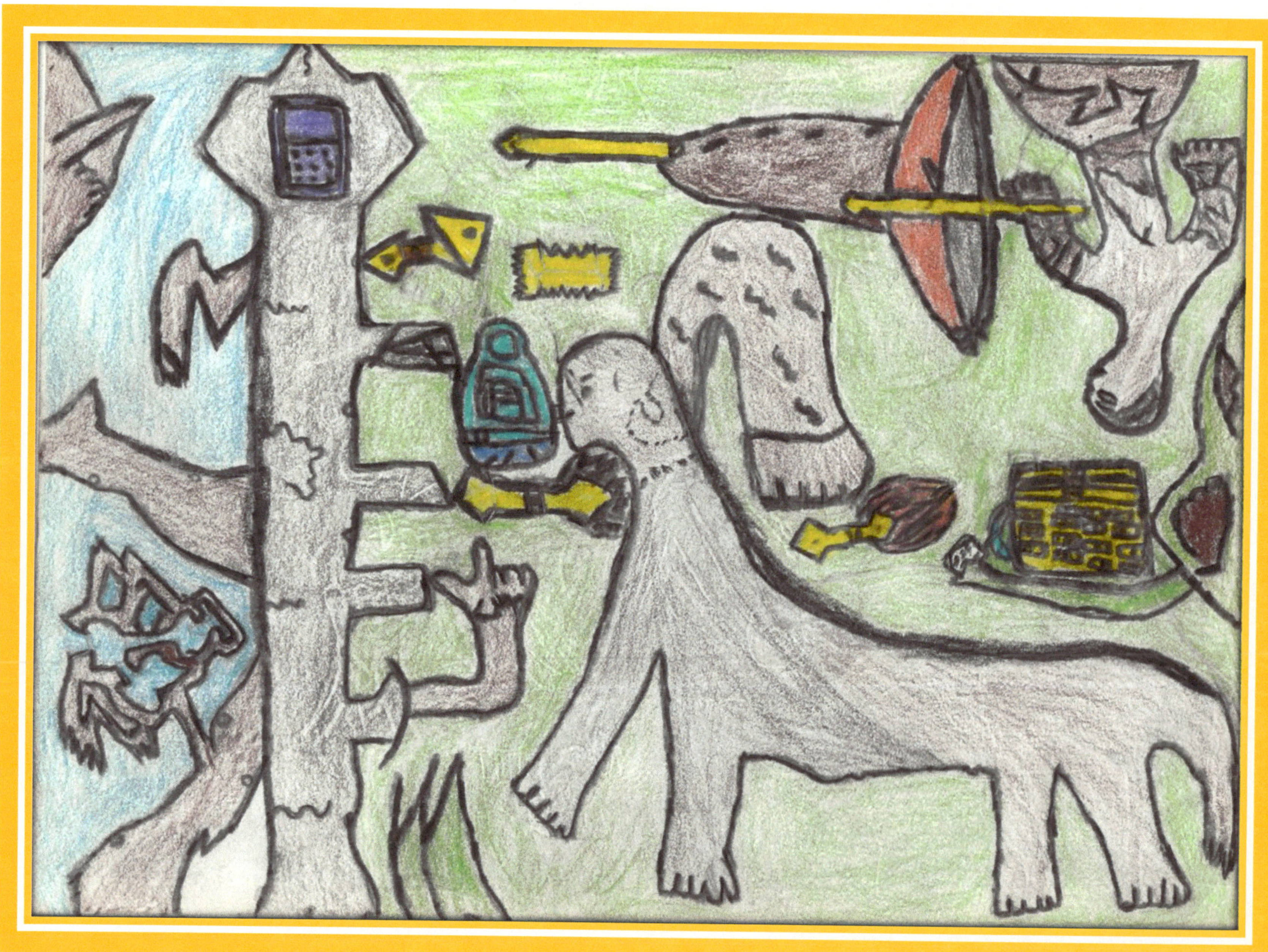

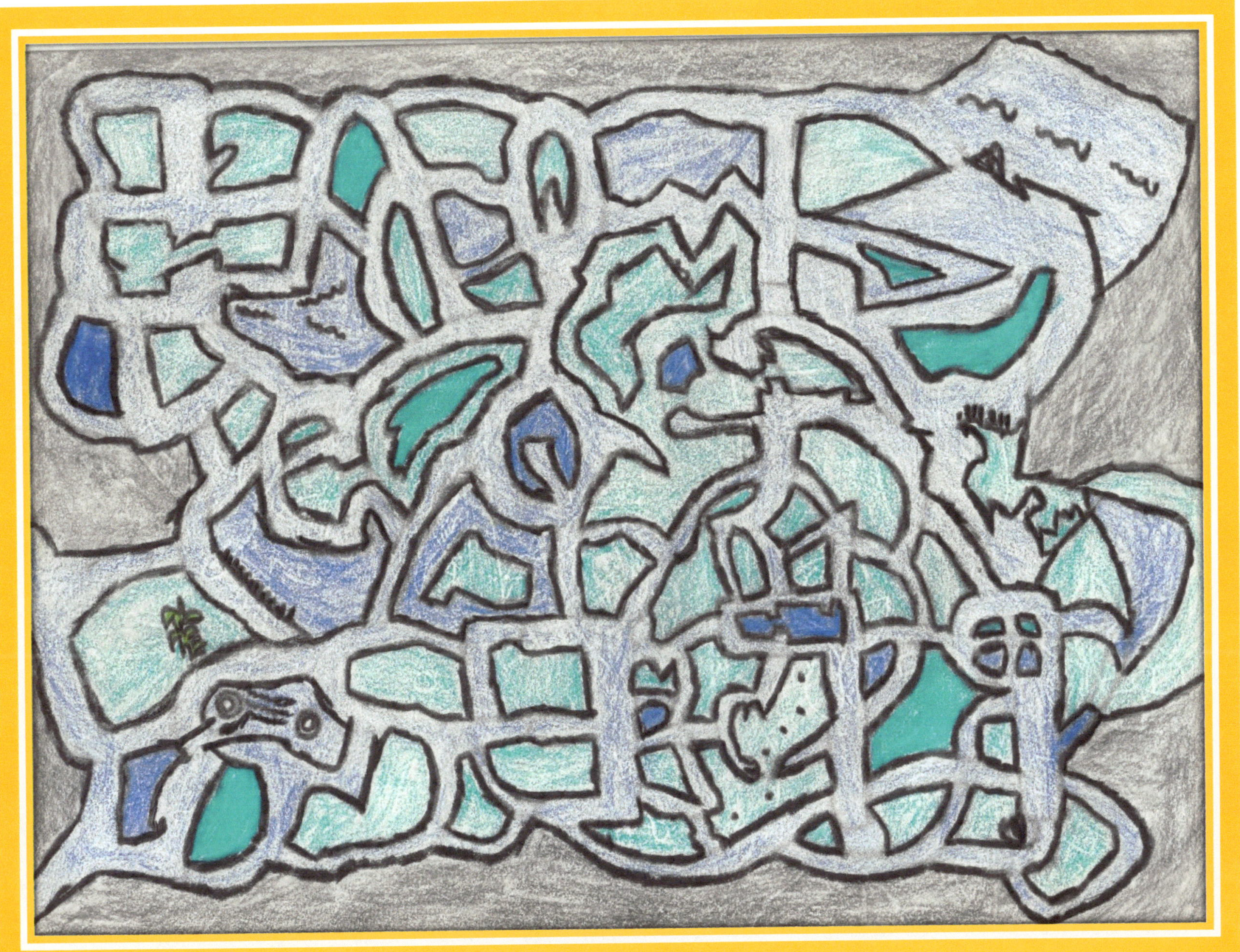

Graphics Band

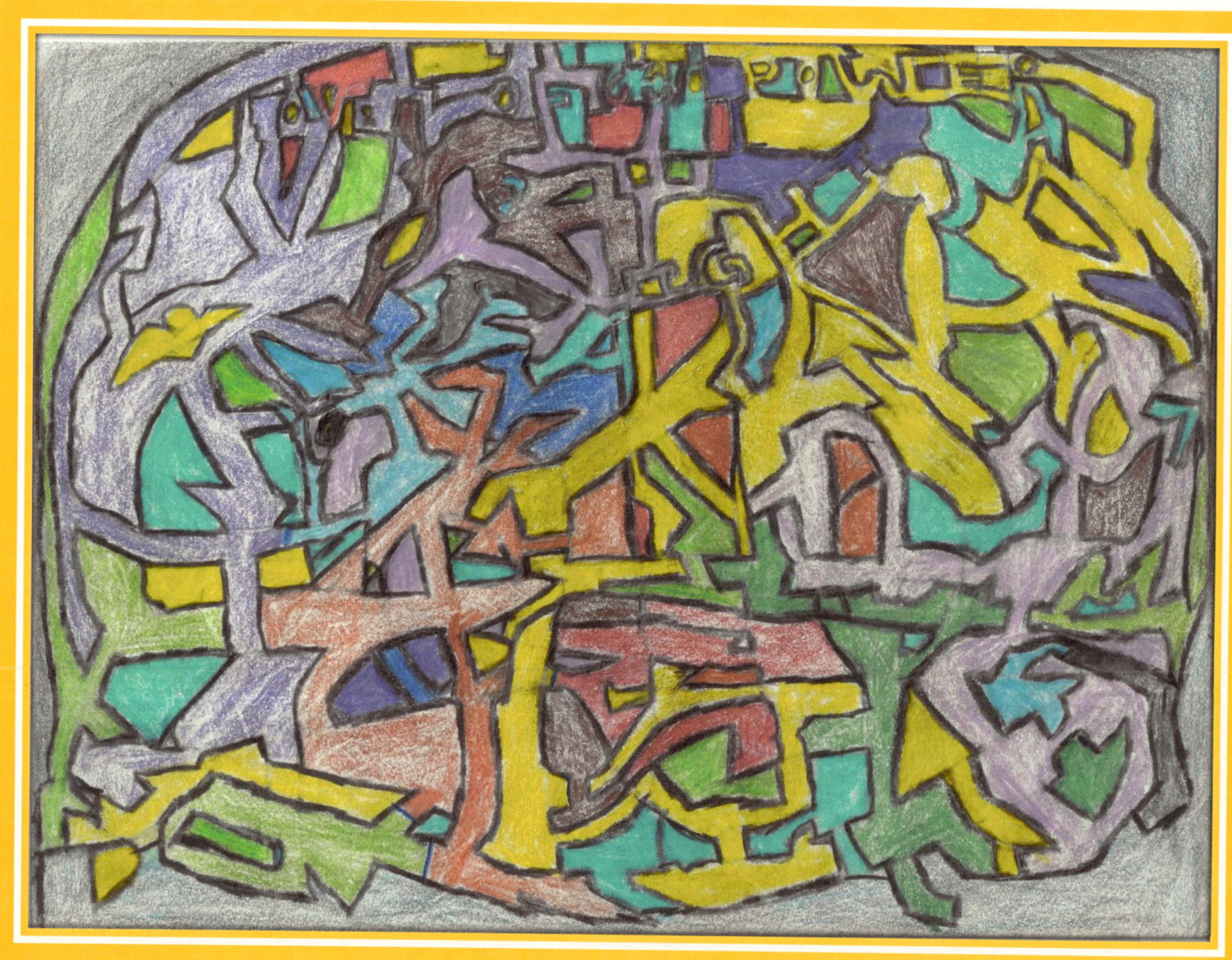

Camille

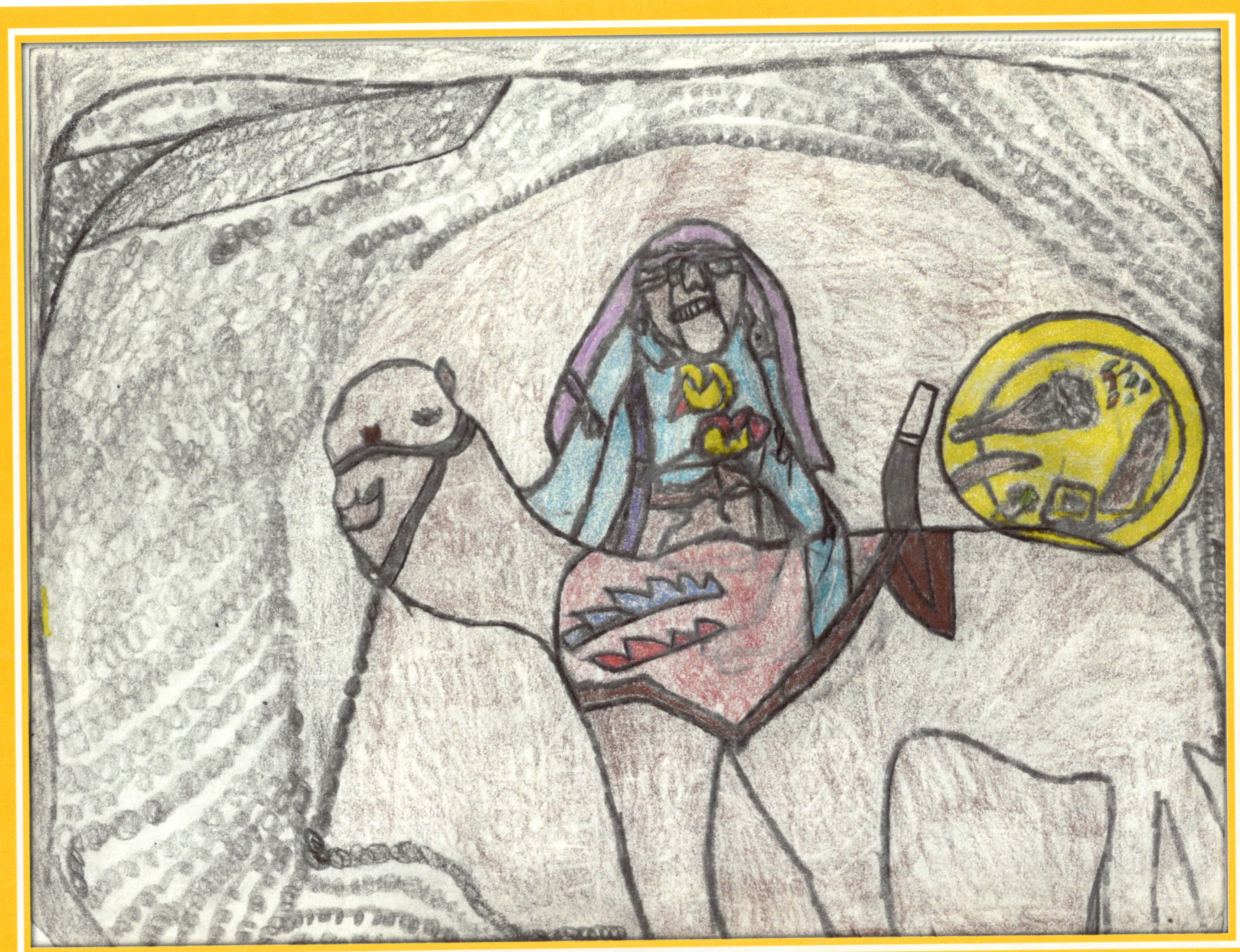

Deers' Palace

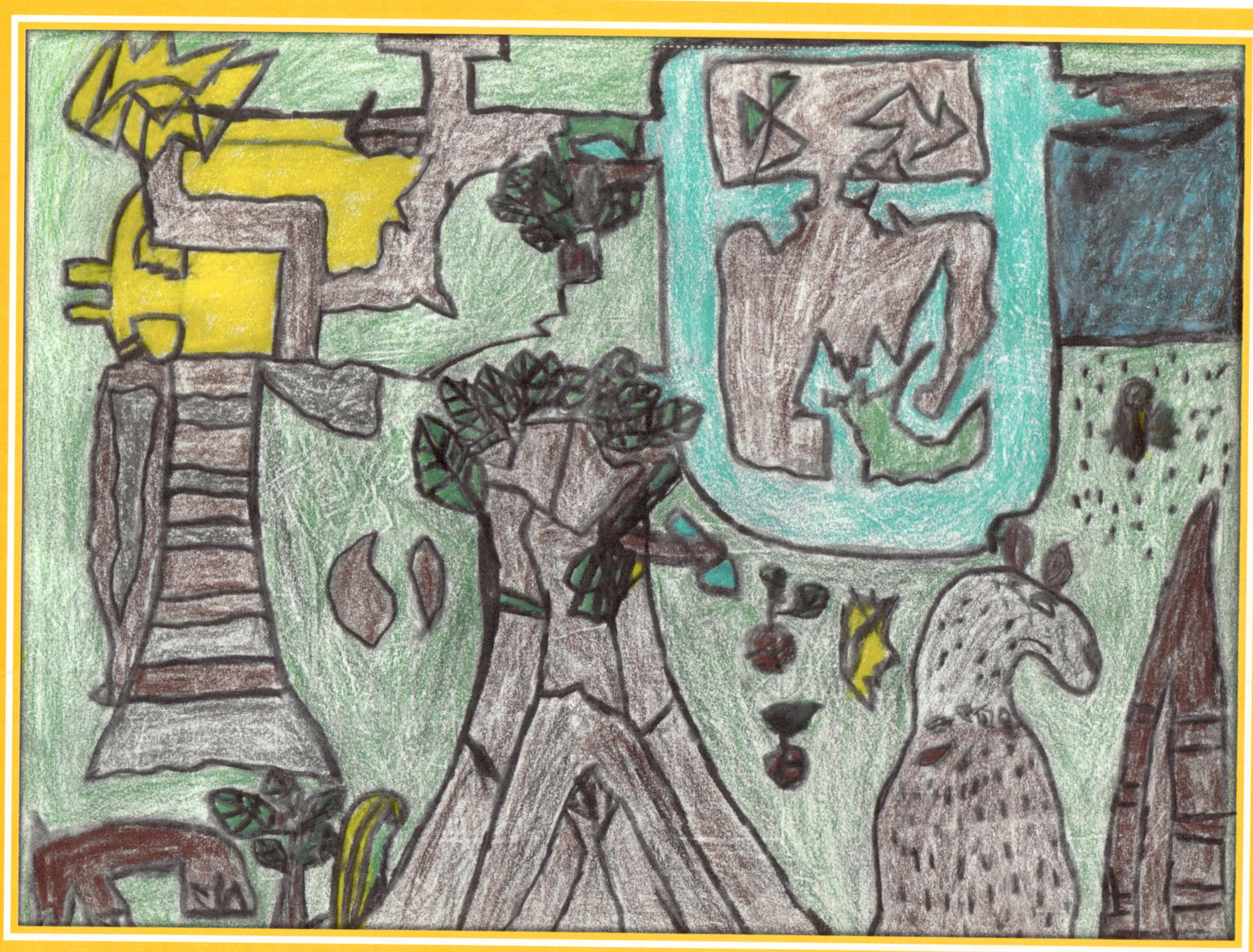

Exclusive

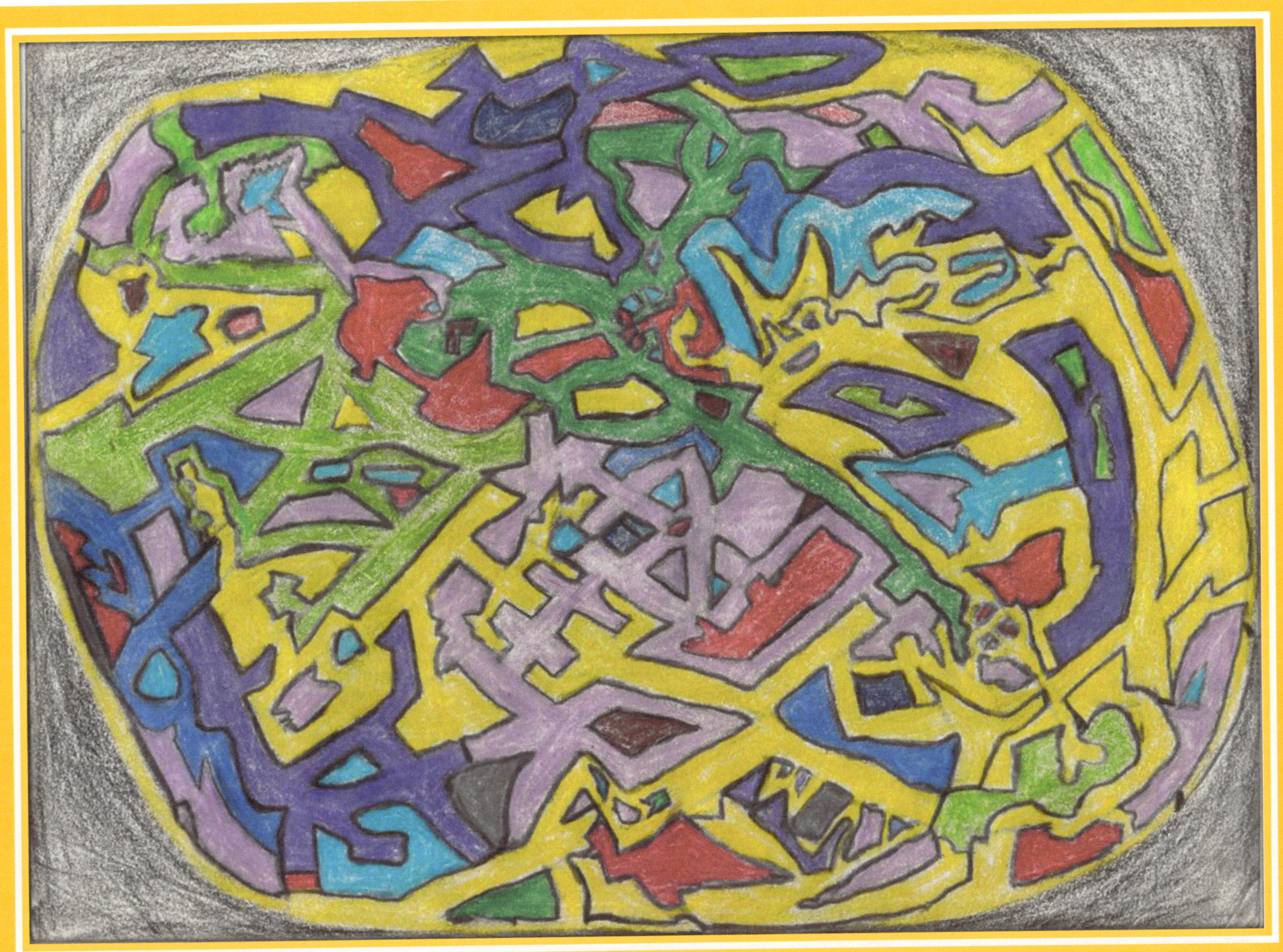

Fill Bill

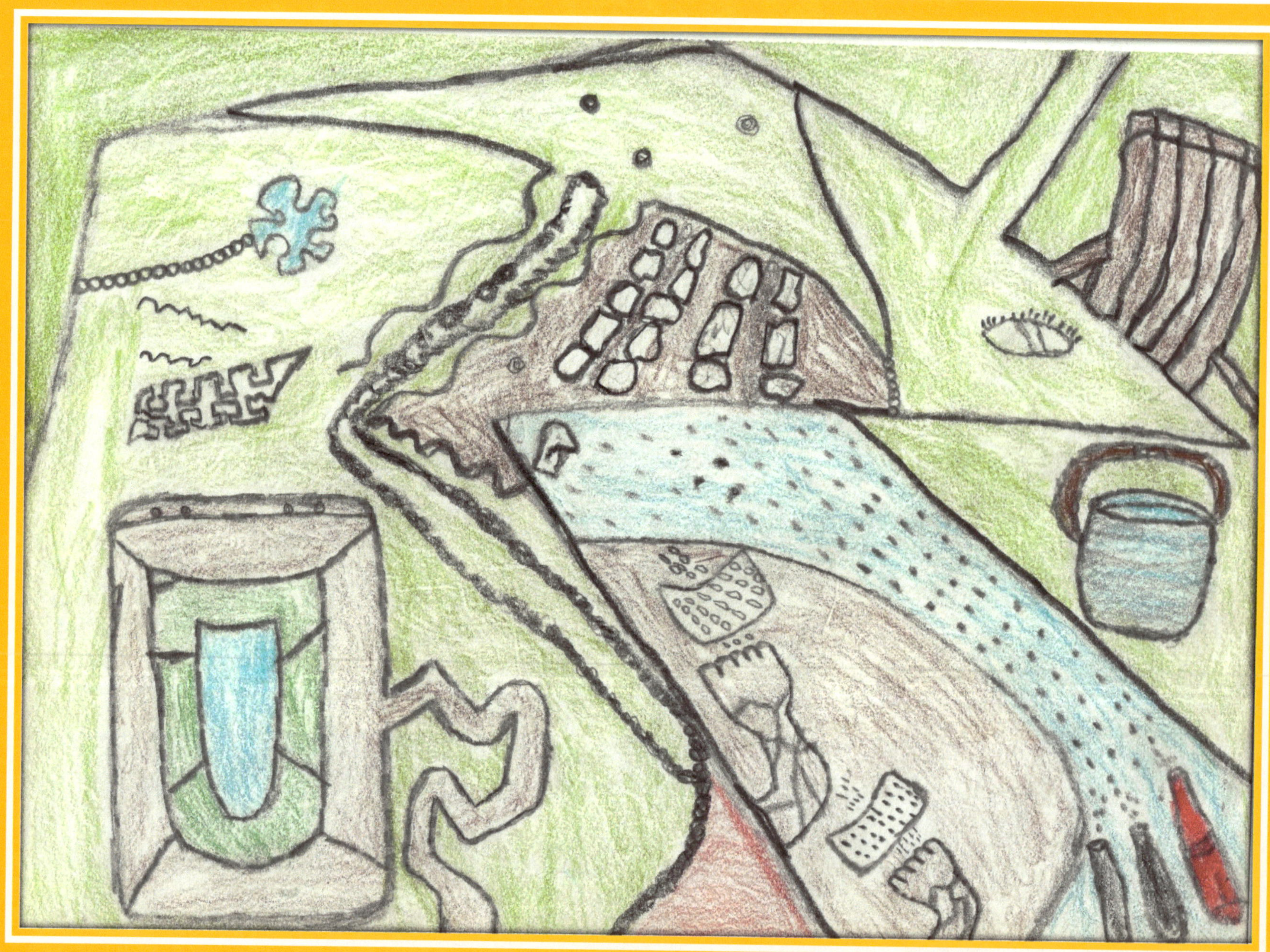

Sports Drive

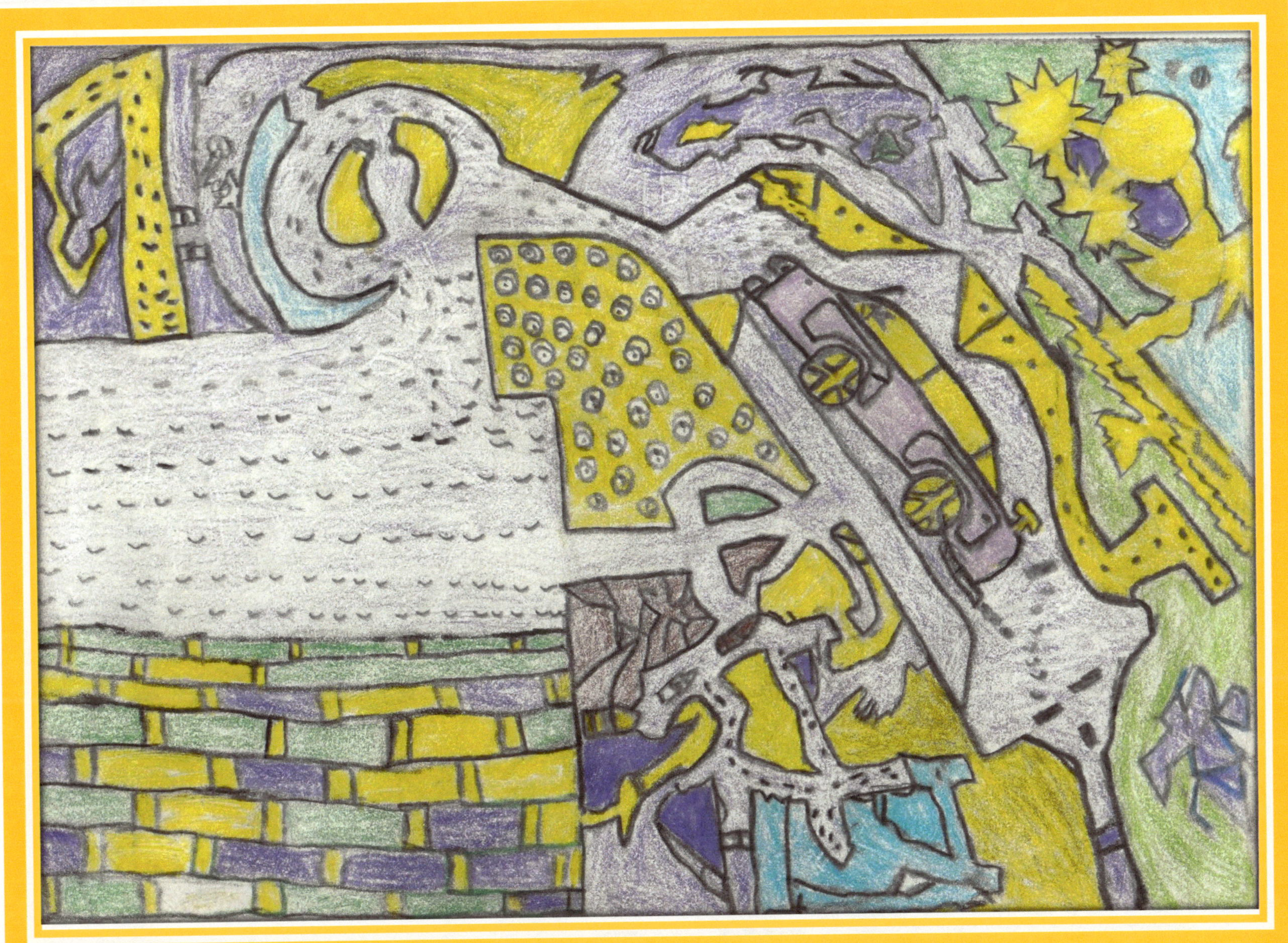

The joy of sports car driving when I used to race cars

Bee's Brat

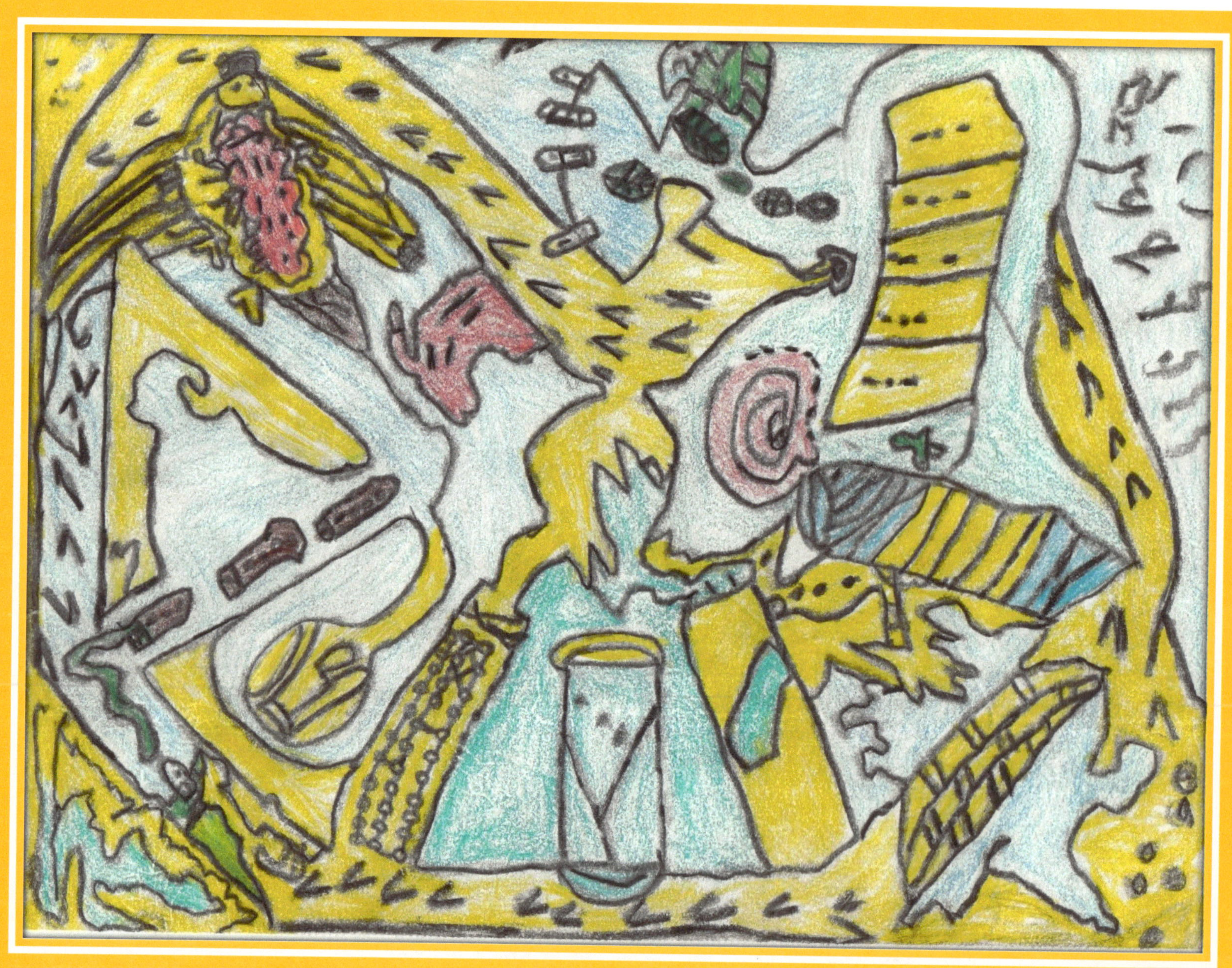

Leg Controller

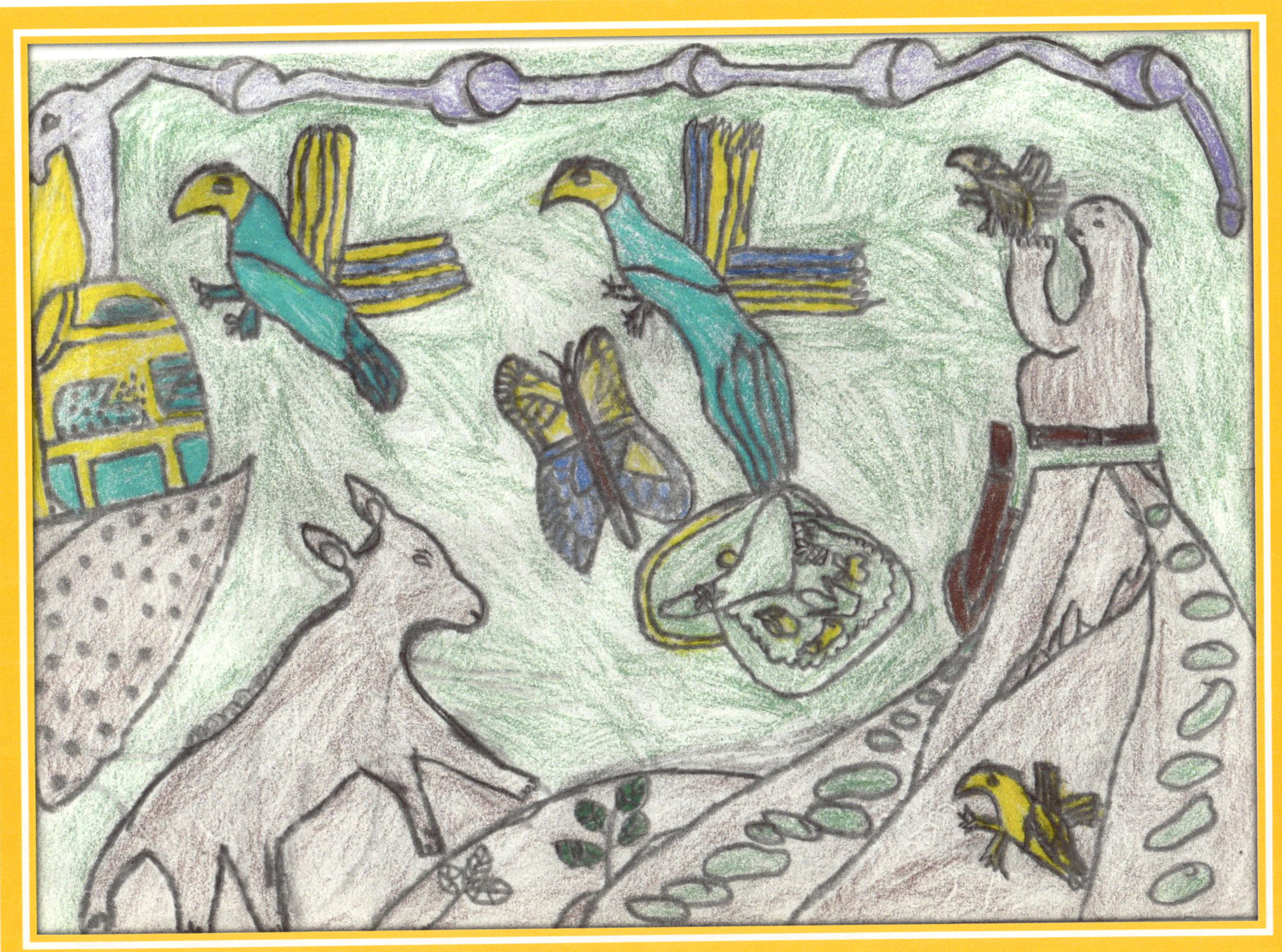

The memory of farm brat knows the way to escape the trap.

Night Vale

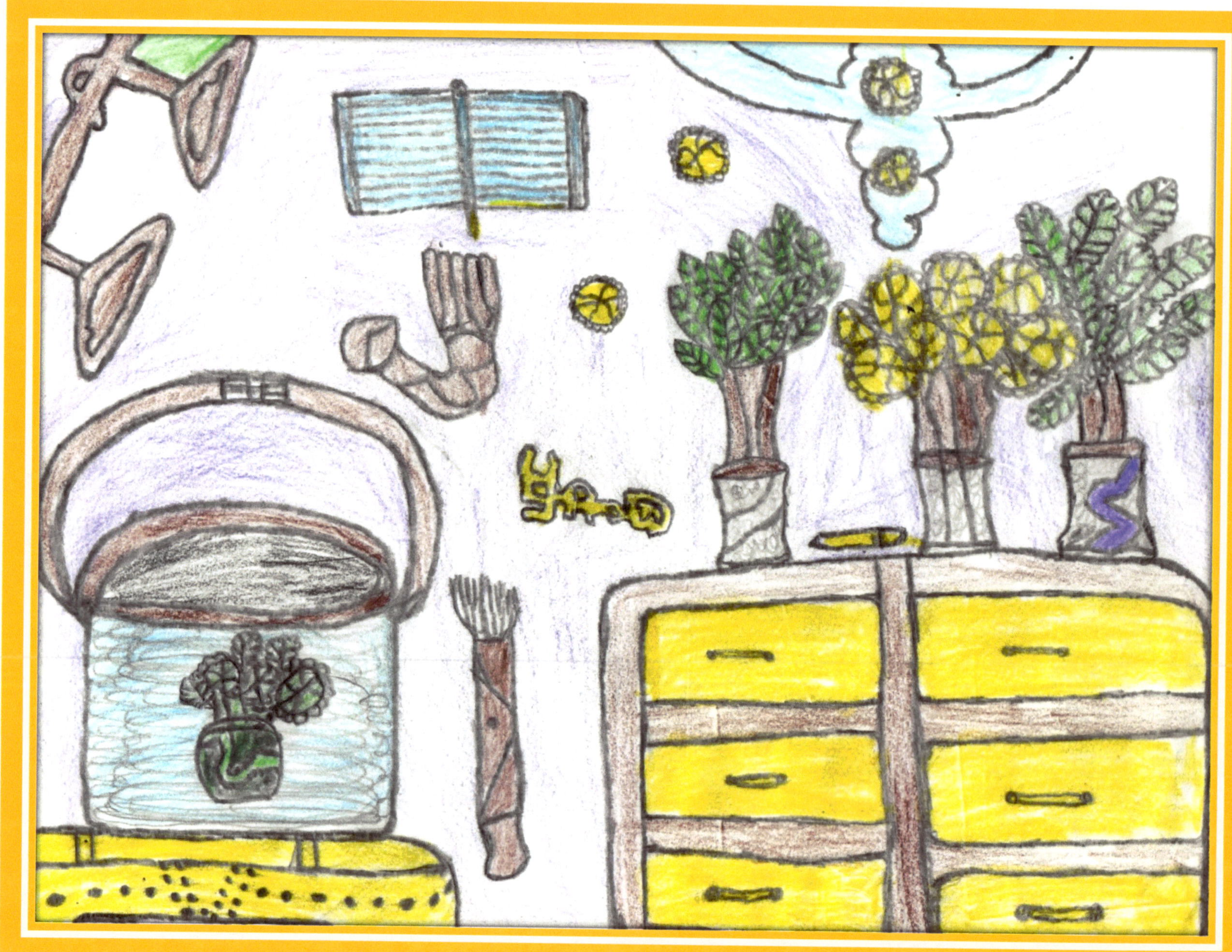

Wave Rain

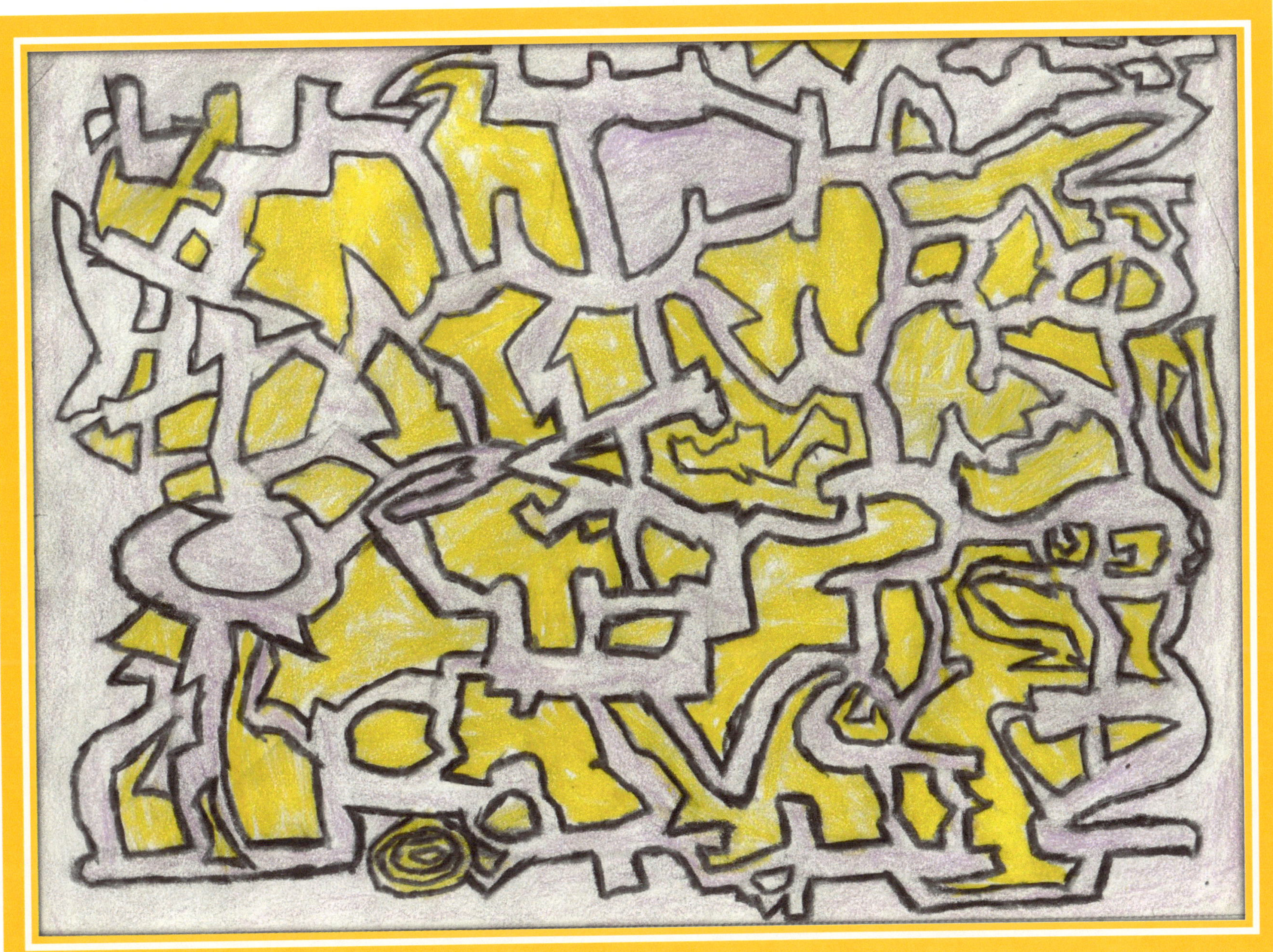

Wild Turn

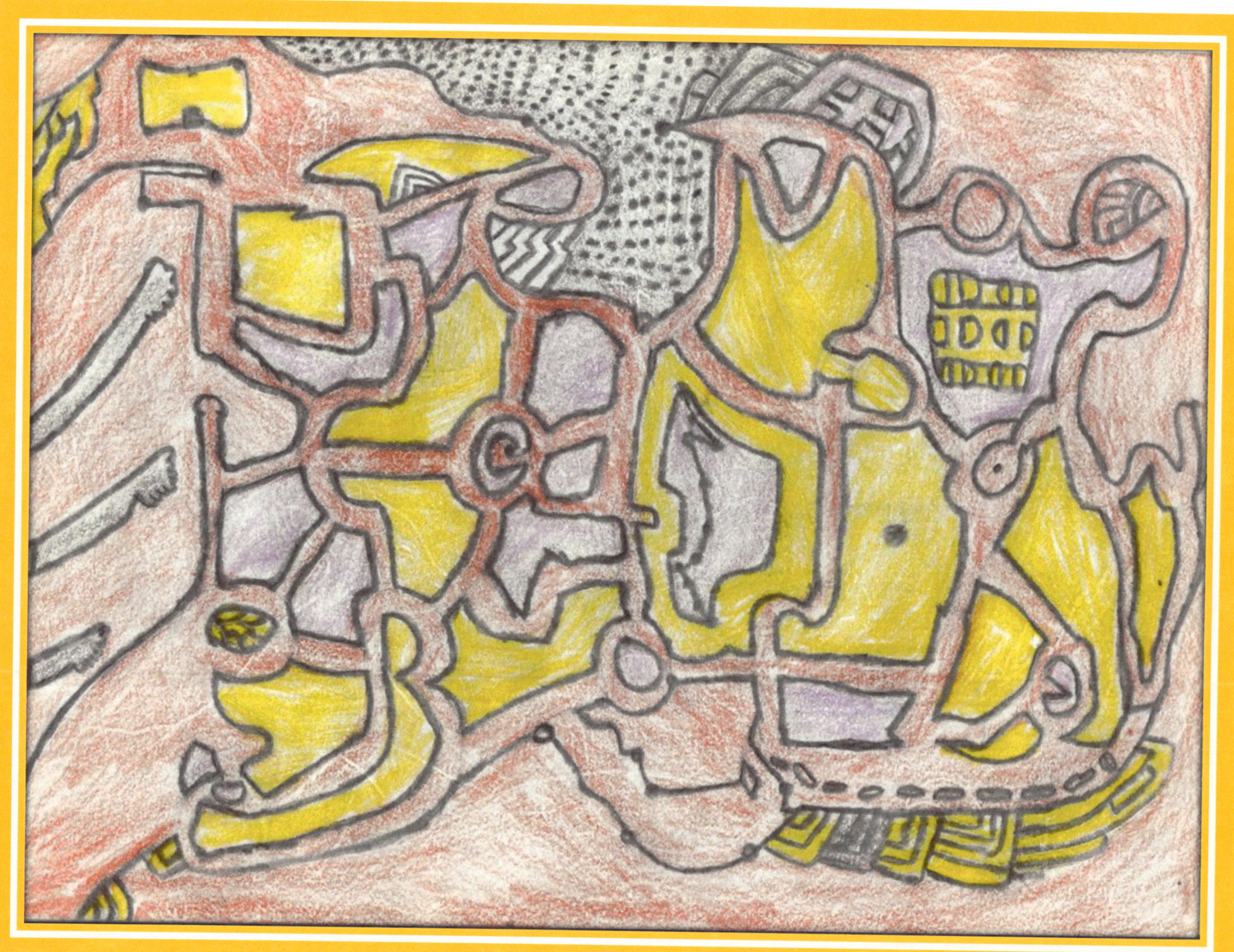

Brave Cattle

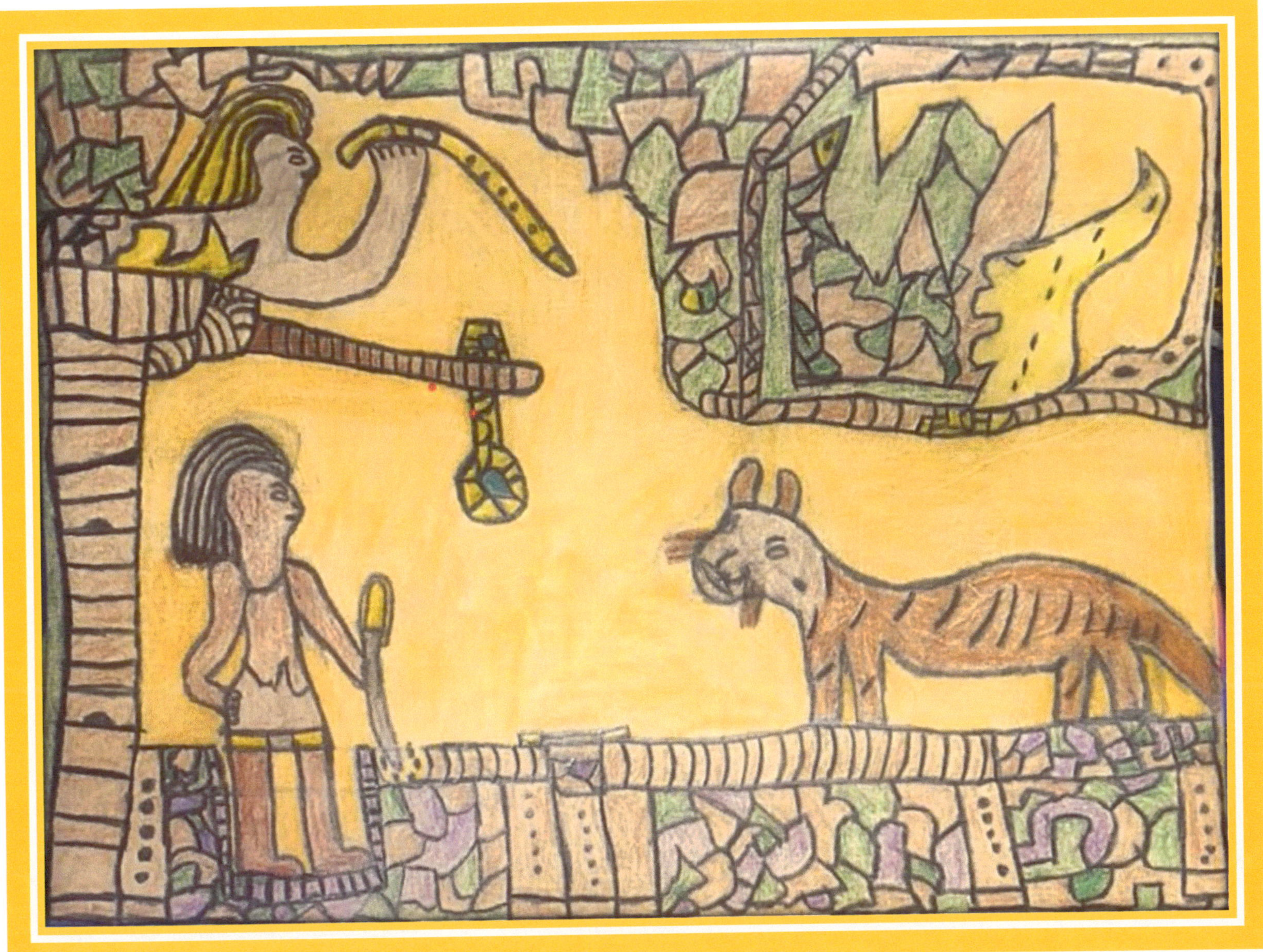

Balancing each other

The End